Back-to-School Chats

Advice from Fathers to their Sons

compiled by

George Bradt

Printed in the United States of America.

For information address:
Durban House Publishing Company, Inc.
7502 Greenville Avenue, Suite 500
Dallas, Texas 75231

Library of Congress Cataloging-in-Publication Data
Bradt, George, YEAR

Back-to-School Chats / George Bradt

Library of Congress Control Number: 2005910148

p. cm.

ISBN 1-930754-87-6
First Edition

10 9 8 7 6 5 4 3 2 1

Visit our Web site at
http://www.durbanhouse.com

Genesis

In September 1999, I was giving my 13-year-old son, Peter, some fatherly advice before he went off to boarding school. I had done something similar the previous year and it seemed to have had the desired impact, so I thought I would try again. Well, that year, after our chat, Peter made me promise to find him or call him up every year, wherever he might be, and give him a "back-to-school chat."

I have honored that promise. By the time you read this, I will have done so at least seven more times. But there's an opportunity for even more. Hence this.

This is Peter's 21st birthday present: a book of back-to-school chats—advice a range of sons have received from their fathers. When the time comes that I am unable to give Peter his back-to-school chat in person, he will have this to refer to.

As long as I'm planning to compile these, why not make them available to others as well? Peter gets the first copy. The rest are up for grabs. If you are reading this, I hope it brings to mind a wonderful back-to-school chat you had with your father.

George Bradt
Peter Bradt's father

Contents

Conditions, Choices and Consequences

Basics

Advice received by Peter Bradt from his father
(September 1998, Tokyo)

As you go off to boarding school for the first
time, remember three things: conditions, choices,
and consequences.

Conditions: There are no conditions attached
to the way I feel about you. I will love you totally
and completely no matter what happens, no
matter what you do. If you do something terrible,
I may be disappointed, but I will never, ever stop
loving you. So, whatever happens, whatever you
do, know that I'm on your side and that you can
always turn to me—without any conditions.

Choices: You always have choices. You may
choose not to choose. You may choose to do what
others tell you to do. You may not like your
choices. But you always have choices. So think
them through and be conscious of the choices
you're making.

Consequences: All choices have consequences. You will make better choices if you think through the potential positive and negative consequences of those choices before you make them.

You are going to make some bad choices. Sometimes you won't understand all the consequences. Sometimes you'll misjudge things. But I'm convinced that if you are consciously making your own choices and thinking through the potential consequences of those choices, you will make far more good choices than if you don't think them through.

So, remember conditions, choices and consequences. Make your own choices after you've thought through the potential consequences. And remember that whether you've made a good choice or a bad choice, there are no conditions on my love for you.

Jorge Silva-Risso, Uruguay

I come from a modest family. The day I started kindergarten, my parents walked with me to the school. They stopped at the gate and before I got in, they told me, "Jorge, if you take advantage of it, your education will be the basis of your success in life." They never gave me any gift to reward my achievements in school. They always said "You're doing this for your own good, not to please us."

And, to be sure, I was always convinced that my success would hinge on my education, and, of course all the efforts were for my own good.

Advice from George L. Williams (father) to George L. Williams II (son), California

My father once told me that human beings sometimes tend to act like herd animals, meaning that they follow trends without thinking because others are doing the same thing. Maybe people feel that there is "safety in numbers" I guess. His point to me was to be very careful in following these types of mass trends, and not to be afraid to act on my own insights... to be my own person. "When you see people doing things out of blind faith... do the opposite or don't participate." His advice has saved me a lot of money in the recent financial market downturn.

Michael Davis, Connecticut

The best advice I ever received from my father was as a high school senior preparing to go to college. He told me that I had to begin right away preparing for a profession. He did not care whether it was a doctor, lawyer, accountant, engineer, etc., but I should study a profession and not even start out in a liberal arts program. Obviously, this had an impact on which schools I applied to, and my choice was accounting. Since my dad was killed in a plane crash when I was a freshman in college, I never got to thoroughly discuss his rationale and the reasons for his attitude, and obviously he never got a chance to see the results. But I believe this was the best advice I ever received from him.

Matt Perry, Massachusetts

Words from my dad: "No drinking and driving. And don't take the jeep on the beach."

Result: drunken driver with a jeep upside-down on the beach below the high water level.

(A good lesson to learn: Listen to what your dad says, before you have to call him the following morning and hear only two more words: "FIX IT!")

Steve Layton, Florida

My father was a great role model for me, mostly through what he did and not what he said. This advice, however, stuck with me because of what was not said. I was in high school and dated one girl for a few months. My dad said, just before I left on a date, "Just remember, Steve, you don't have to marry her." That was it on sex from my dad. What he didn't say was, be responsible and I trust you. I got the message. I don't think that women, like my wife, understand this from a male perspective.

George

Richard A. Karwic, Connecticut

A couple of pearls of wisdom come to my
mind in terms of "fatherly advice."

The first has to do with advice I gave my four
sons about choices and decision making. One of
Newton's Laws of Physics is that "to every action
there is an equal and opposite reaction." I just took
it one step further to behavior and child rearing. I
always emphasized to my sons that life is a series
of decisions (actions) and in order to make good
decisions, they needed to learn and understand the
consequences of their decisions (reactions). Then
decide (choose).

Choosing, decision making, and understanding consequences (both good and undesir-
able) was a constant theme in our house.

At an early age, they learned that if they stayed
up too late in the evening, then they would find
themselves tired the next day. If they hurt
someone, expect to get hurt back. More impor-
tantly, if they were nice to someone, expect that
person to be nice to you, and maybe feel good
about yourself. If they spent their allowance on
many little spontaneous purchases, there would be
no savings accumulated for large purchases. If
they worked hard in school and got good grades,
they would be rewarded. Etc.

A practical example of how this was applied
would be in our rule about playing baseball in the

backyard. Most fathers would get nervous about their sons playing baseball in a small backyard. (All those windows!) I never told my sons they could not play baseball in the backyard. I simply told my sons that if they wished to play baseball in the yard, then they had assumed responsibility for the well-being of our house's windows. The phrase was "every window has a price." If you break a window (action), then you will buy the replacement window from your allowance (reaction). The choice: "play at home and risk breaking a window, or walk to the park, and play safe." Some days they took the risk. Some days they took the walk. In thirty years, I only replaced one window. (At that, it was an inexpensive cellar window). There was no reprimand, no punishment, no being grounded, no criticism. I simply handed them the bill for the glass, and out came the allowance funds.

Another piece of advice has to do with dispelling the myth that "boys will be boys." That is nonsense! Those words are usually spoken by fathers regarding mistakes, misbehaviors, or other poor actions of their sons. The advice I was given was that "boys will be young gentlemen."

Being well mannered, properly disciplined, and respectful of others has nothing to do with gender. Fathers who are failing to properly raise young gentlemen usually start the process well before the child understands gender, so the "boys will be boys" excuse does not hold water.

Lloyd Hansen, North Dakota

My dad told me if you do something you love, it won't seem like work. I took that advice. Although I grew up on a farm in North Dakota, I became an accountant. A high school teacher introduced me to accounting and it was like a light turned on inside me. I've been one now for over thirty-five years and go to "work" each day with a sense of excitement and anticipation. It sure doesn't seem like work.

As my children were growing up, I taught that same principle to them. One of my sons always walked around with a pencil in his hand drawing, doodling or illustrating something (my wall, my window, my book). Today, he is a graphics designer doing Web design work and beta testing new graphics software. Another son used to come home, sit on his bed and read the paper from front to back. Today, he is a reporter for a major newspaper in California. A daughter got involved in practically every social cause available in high school—walks for cancer, teaching mentally challenged children, rape victims counseling. Today she works for a Washington, DC, non-profit organization dedicated to improving the health and safety of women, children, and families. Another daughter now is studying nutrition and childcare in college. She has been taking care of children in church since sixth grade, and she comes home at night and spends 2-3 hours in the kitchen practicing cooking. All of them are doing something they love, and three of them are even getting paid for it.

Letter from Jamie Cornehlson to his Father, June 18, 2004, New York

Thirty-three years ago today (Father's Day) you became a father. You e-mailed me a few weeks back about remembrances of our parents or grandparents. On this, your 33rd Father's Day, I have a few. You were invincible. I always looked up to you thinking that you could do anything you put your mind to. I remember going to Mohawk, that lump of dirt in Connecticut, to go skiing, except on this day we were a little late getting on the slopes. Not because we were late. We were always the first ones on the lift and the last ones off. Even if that meant frostbite. We were delayed because you were studying the design of the covered bridge at Mohawk so you could build a bridge for the house on Green Beach Drive. You weren't an engineer or a carpenter but you decided to build it. Last time I checked it was still there.

I also remember driving back with Fred Grey from whitewater rafting in Pennsylvania. The VW bus they had broke down outside of New Jersey. All I could remember as we tried to get back home was that I wished you were here because you would know what to do to get us out of this mess.

Well, that brings me to what I took away from all this. I have a lasting impression that if you could do anything you put your mind to, then I can do just the same. It's not like I had a choice—you basically burned that into my conscious.

Well, it is now time to prove that I can do anything I want to. I have enclosed my business plan. Your help and insight would be much appreciated. Please do not hold back on the tough questions or criticism. The whole point of this exercise is to clear up any hurdles now before I pull the trigger and launch the product.

Have a great Father's Day.
Jamie

Learning is life's blood. *Neal Greene, California*

Think independently. *Steve Shyung, China*

It's not important if you know it. What's important is if you know where to find it. *Dan Kelly's grandfather, August Seher, Georgia*

Education is the one thing nobody can take away from you. *Scott Ewart, England*

My father was strong on "people must live their own lives." Too bad he seemed able to apply it to everyone except me! *Roger Neill, England*

Notice and Appreciate

People

Advice received by Peter Bradt from his father (September 1999, Taipei)

As you settle in to your second year at Winchester, make sure you're noticing and appreciating all that you're experiencing. It's a great place, filled with all sorts of great things. You will pass them by unless you make the choice to notice and appreciate them.

Notice what's going on around you. Notice the people in the school and around the school—the teachers, the staff, the students, the community members. Notice what activities you and others are engaged in. Or not engaged in. Notice the choices you're making, remembering that choosing not to choose is a choice in itself. Notice how you feel about things. Notice with all your senses.

And appreciate all the great things that happen to you. Take the time to soak them in, to make memories. Appreciate the impact you have on others and how you add to their lives. People really enjoy being around you. Another way of saying that is to say that you bring joy to people. And that's a gift. So appreciate it. Appreciate all the good things others do for you: the teachers, the staff, your peers.

You're about to have a wonderful, relatively pressure-free year. Make sure you milk it for all it's worth. Make sure you notice and appreciate how wonderful it is.

Mike Crosby, California

I have a short story about working with my dad. My dad owned a small auto parts store for many years. One of his many duties was to call on repair shops and take stock orders for various auto parts lines.

When I turned eighteen years old, my father decided that it was time for me to take over this duty. We traveled to a shop and he told me to ask the owner what he needed this week. Upon doing so the owner informed us that his stock was fine and he really did not need anything. We went to the next shop and again I was told that they did not need anything. I walked back to the car feeling a little rejected, and my dad said he would take the next one.

When we arrived at the next shop my dad walked around back and started digging through the trash dumpster. Needless to say, I was completely astonished and a little embarrassed. My dad pulled out three empty air filter boxes and some used spark plugs.

He walked into the office and asked the owner what he needed. The owner told my dad that they did not need anything. I actually started to smile, knowing that the old veteran was turned down as well.

My dad pulled out the boxes and spark plugs

and told the owner that he noticed these empty boxes around and would be more than happy to replace them so they will have them when needed. The owner said sure and apologized for not looking.

When we were taking the order the mechanics were complaining about a diagnostic tool that had broken. Upon leaving with order in hand my dad told the owner that he would send over a tool catalog so they could look into replacing the broken one. The owner said don't bother, just send the new tool.

The original "no" turned into a $3000 order, and with very little being said I learned two very valuable lessons. First of all, do not take no for an answer. Secondly, the customers do not always know what they need and it is my job to teach them. Thanks, Dad!

Kelly Mankin, Michigan

A dear friend's father just passed away, and I got to know him during the last nine months of his life. He was suffering from congestive heart failure, which prevented him from doing much physical activity, and he knew it was degenerative, that he would just get worse as the days passed.

I loved his attitude. Through all the frustrating medications, hospital stays and just being short of breath from going to the bathroom, he always had a smile on his face and would say classic lines like "most people my age are dead," or, "what the hell, it could be worse."

Most of all, he believed in being a good person first. He always used to say to me that "my mother taught me to be nice to people; being mean doesn't get you anywhere and will make you a cynic. If you take care of people you'll be paid back ten-fold."

And you know what? He was right. His son took such good care of him during those last few months and gave him comfort that he couldn't possibly have known through strangers.

I'm blessed to have known that old man at a time in my life when it would be easy to become cynical. And I'm blessed to be close to the son who would do that for his father.

Antonio Leung, Hong Kong

A FRIEND—The little boy and the fence.

There was a little boy with a bad temper. His father gave him a bag of nails and told him that every time he lost his temper, he should hammer a nail into the back fence. The first day, the boy had 37 nailed into the fence. Then it gradually dwindled down. He discovered it was easier to hold his temper than to drive those nails into the fence.

Finally the day came when the boy didn't lose his temper at all. He told his father about it, and the father suggested that the boy now pull out one nail for each day that he was able to hold his temper.

The days passed, and the young boy was finally able to tell his father that all the nails were gone. The father took his son by the hand and led him to the fence.

He said, "You have done well, my son, but look at the holes in the fence. The fence will never be the same. When you say things in anger, they leave a scar just like this one. You can put a knife into a man and draw it out. It won't matter how many times you say I'm sorry. The wound is still there. A verbal wound is as bad as a physical one."

Friends are a very rare jewel, indeed. They make you smile and encourage you to succeed.

They lend an ear, they share a word of praise, and they always want to open their hearts to us.

Chris Lin, Taiwan

This is what my father told me at my age of eleven when I went to junior high boarding school. I try my best translate it in English.

Life which is one continuous struggle with other men is hardly worth living. Under this unavoidable scenario, maturity is fraught with all sorts of pain and bitterness. It does give you rare opportunity to connect with people. Keep doing that, it eventually leads to the pleasure (success) of being a human being.

I was extremely introvert at that point in time, and this advice always encouraged me up to my adulthood.

Matt Doherty, North Carolina

When I was in fourth grade, my dad had just bought me my first jock at Nescott Drugs as he was getting ready to send me to Gus Alfieri's All-American Basketball Camp on Long Island. We were sitting in the car and he said, "When a coach is telling you something, don't interrupt and say 'I know.' Let him finish what he wants to tell you." In other words, listen and you just might learn something.

Bert C. Hensley, California

A long time ago, I was dating a woman with whom I was madly in love. She was beautiful, brilliant, well read, well educated, a good athlete, and she spoke seven languages. I thought she was the best thing I would ever find.

Unfortunately, she was often sullen and even difficult to be around. She really never seemed satisfied. My father said that while he liked her and understood why I loved her so much, he had concerns. He said, "My experience has been that if someone doesn't love themselves, they really can't love anyone else." He was absolutely right. Although I loved this woman, she could never really love me in return until she learned to love herself.

Also...

The best advice my father ever gave me was "Someone who can't trust cannot be trusted." The most difficult personal and management challenges that I have had have been with people who cannot trust. They cause you to waste so much time because you have to constantly explain the logic for your actions instead of focusing on resolving issues and improving things, you end up burning resources constantly explaining to them why a particular decision was made. The reason is because they have ulterior motives, they assume that others do as well. At the end of the day you cannot trust someone who is incessantly questioning your every move and it is simply better to just get them out of your life. You cannot convince someone who has a poverty of spirit to suddenly trust you and your actions. You end up throwing an enormous amount of energy down a bottomless pit. I had to learn and relearn this lesson a few times, but I think I finally get it now.

Nat Stoddard, New York

The best advice I ever received from my father was instructions on how to shake hands. I was ten years old, and he and I were having lunch together. He said, "When you go to shake hands with someone, extend your arm, plant both feet squarely on the ground, look at his hand just long enough to insure that you grasp it fully so your thumbs are engaged, look him in the eyes and say your name clearly." Then to prove that it works, upon leaving the restaurant, he walked up to a total stranger, stuck out his hand and introduced himself... you would have thought they were long-lost friends by the way in which the stranger responded. A very impressive, memorable and useful piece of advice for this ten-year old to receive.

Mike Hsieh, Japan

Tamara is a skilled fisherman in the village of Mylos. When his son, Aki, reached the age of eight, Tamara decided it was time to teach Aki the invaluable skill of fishing. After waking the boy up before dawn and paddling out into the middle of the bay, he started to show Aki how to untangle the net. Soon the sun would rise and it would be a fine day for fishing, thought Tamara to himself.

"Dad," asked Aki as they were almost done with the nets, "what were you afraid of when you were a child?"

This question somewhat took Tamara by surprise, for he was hoping Aki would ask about fishing during this expedition. Nevertheless, Tamara had encouraged Aki to ask questions and promised always to answer him truthfully. "Well, I used to be afraid of monsters under my bed in the middle of the night. When I was frightened I would climb into my parents' bed and fall asleep between them."

"What were you afraid of when you became an adult?" inquired his son.

This took a little bit of reflection as Tamara wanted to give his son a thoughtful answer. "When I became an adult in the village, my greatest fear was that I would fail in my chosen craft, which was fishing."

A moment of silence passed as Aki looked up to his father again and asked, "Dad, what are you afraid of now?"

Now this question stumped Tamara, for nobody had ever asked him this before. It was not even a question he had dared ask himself. As his mind raced while his hands worked on the net, Tamara fumbled for an answer and finally came up with one.

"If my life were to end today, my greatest fear would be to discover that the people that I cared for most in the world did not love me," Tamara said aloud. He looked at Aki and could detect no reaction from his son. At once Tamara felt a pang of regret. His statement sounded selfish and small-minded.

"I take that back," said Tamara, "if my life were to end today, my greatest fear would be that I failed to give as much love as I could have given in this lifetime." This time his statement struck him like a lightning bolt. Tamara felt flushed with emotion, reminding him of the time when he knew he would marry his wife or when his child was born. He recognized it as a moment of truth.

Turning his head, Tamara could see his son nodding at him. "And I thought I was the teacher today," smiled Tamara to himself. That day they returned with a great catch. It was a magnificent day for fishing.

Two years ago, this conversation actually occurred between my son and I while we were alone in our home. It basically summarizes where I am today, still trying to switch from a mentality of seeking love to giving love. I am blessed with a loving wife, Tonia, and two wonderful children, Karina and Mason, along with a great career. Yet I still fight a natural inclination to hoard when already I have so much. That's the essence of my personal journey and the real story of my life.

Jim Rowbotham, New York

My father, Brigadier General J.H. Rowbotham (1911-1996), administered "concise advice," along with carefully selected reading material, to me:

• His favorite acronym-aphorism was "R.T.P. Read The Problem." That went for math, or business, or everyday life. If you don't understand whatever you're facing, you'll produce the wrong answer/solution.

• He would periodically buy me books that I now realize were prescient. One, when I was in prep school, was a biography of the original Charles Schwab, long-time Chairman of Bethlehem Steel. When Schwab retired, Bethlehem Steel started its decline. Another was *Pacific Islands Speaking*, by journalist Armstrong Sperry, which was a Christmas gift when I was maybe eleven years old (I enjoyed reading early on). This book was prophetic, profiling nations like Singapore, the Philippines and, yes, Japan as emerging forces in the global economy.

• As a frustrated architect (he earned his degree in architecture from Princeton in 1932, at the nadir of the Depression), he transferred his visual arts skills to marketing with Atlantic Richfield (interrupted by six years' WW II active duty, including combat in the Philippines). His freehand charts and graphs, rendered on white cardboard for presentations, were astoundingly precise and lucid.

When my sister and I visit our mother and him at Arlington National Cemetery, which we did last month along with my wife Cindy, the above are part of our memories of a true Main Line Philadelphia gentleman, a caring father, and a war hero.

Randy Johnson, New York

Robert E. Johnson
Schenectady, New York
Saturday Morning
March 13, 1965

Dear Son,

Tomorrow marks an important milestone for you—you attain "legal age." Having been through this I can assure you that you will feel no different—and be no wiser or stronger—next week than you were last week. Nevertheless, there is a difference, because it marks another change in the gradually increasing independence you have and a corresponding decrease in the dependence on your parents. There is only one more big step and perhaps two in this changing relationship—your becoming self-supporting and later—I hope—married—in that order.

The tone of this letter is intended to reflect my recognition of your maturity because anything I say will be received only on its own merit and not because it's your father talking.

Your ideas about life and moral values are already well established, but you should recognize that you are still impressionable. So think carefully before you make important decisions or actions, be they educational, business or social. Remember that the really intelligent people never hesitate to ask for advice from those they respect and trust. The really strong people do not feel inferior because they seek counsel and the intelligent people seem to sense a good and reliable source for critical appraisal and comment. I mention this because you will have fewer occasions to turn automatically to your parents as you grow older. Naturally, I hope we'll always be able to discuss things of concern to both of us, but I'm recognizing that this is a matter increasingly for your decision.

The following comments relate to a concern of mine about the overall family relationships. Here again this will be a matter for your own decision. In a family I hope that concern for each other is a natural—perhaps instinctive—reaction. If you have any feelings at all, I wish that you would show at least some recognition to your sisters. The slightest attention is so important because they look up to you. In this matter time is very short—perhaps too short—and unless there is a recognition now it would seem doubtful there ever will be, and I believe there would be a loss to all. I say this not in the sense that things would be necessarily bad, but in the sense that future relationships could be richer and better and meaningful and helpful.

Well, enough philosophizing. We hope you received the cake on time and that you're enjoying the day. Also, I hope you have a good vacation. I'm planning to go to San Jose on the 21st of March and will be gone the following week. Do you know what your plans will be?

Sue is home for the weekend and has been fine. She seems to really enjoy being home and has been helping around the house.

Have to go now, but I want to close by just saying

Happy birthday,

Dad

P.S. A birthday check is enclosed.

John Courtis, England

It's a long time ago, but he turned experience getting his last job into basic advice for me. He had after some years in post asked diffidently of his new boss, the top banana at Sanwa Bank of Osaka, London office, why they had chosen him rather than the other extremely good candidates to be their senior Brit, i.e. London Advisor. "Because, Tom, you spoke so slowly and clearly we could understand every word!" Actually, he may also have been emulating his successful stage role as the Mikado...

This excellent principle I follow still, if I don't get too excited! On reflection, Noel Coward too told young actors, "Speak clearly and don't fall over the furniture."

All Tom's other good advice that I can recall related to restaurants, wine and food...or parade ground drill. Or the condition on which he was prepared to answer questions in the home—not competing with the radio, television or third party babble!

Dan Kelley, Georgia

I have two that I can recall handily:

He said to me when I was about 17 or 18 years old, "Do your best to stay away from the girls." My father, who married young, had seven children in ten years and never had two nickels to rub together, was trying to advise me not to be in a hurry to get married or to "create a situation" in which I would "have to get married."

I heard, but didn't really listen. I married young and got divorced, but I have two wonderful children to show for it and I know a lot more about being married as a result.

He often said, "Do something. Even if it is not right, it is bound to be better than nothing at all." I will never forget this one and try to apply it to our business every day.

P.S. I have an eleven-year-old son. The simplest and most sound advice I give him is to "respect yourself and respect others in everything you do." I figure that pretty well covers all the bases! I also ask him frequently what he is proud of himself. I reckon it is at least as important that he is proud of himself than it is for me to be proud of him.

Mose Hazo, Connecticut

I have four sons, all now in their thirties and fortunately doing well. As they were growing up, there were a few fundamentals preached constantly to them as soon as they were old enough to understand:

• Love one another. You may disagree but no one will ever care more consistently about you than family.

• Always care for your mother (assumption that Dad will predecease Mom).

• From your talents, give back to others.

• Be fair, ethical, and considerate of others.

• Set a standard for yourself and strive toward it rather having others setting your standards.

How did these apply in practice?

• From the first in college to the last, the boys conference called so they could stay in touch without us knowing until the phone bills came in.

• To this day, the boys and their families are up to the minute despite living in New Hampshire, Massachusetts, Connecticut and California.

• All of them and their families gathered to celebrate their mom's birthday, providing a vacation and diamond earrings for her.

Thankfully all of our sons are decent, honorable young men who are excellent fathers, husbands and tireless executives who are ethical. Each has created his own goals and standards which are accepted by each despite any differences.

What particularly stands out? This story could be any of the boys (now men), but I will use our second son as an example.

Peter was a fine student in a quality high school and then accepted to some excellent colleges. During his college days, he volunteered to help children in Appalachia with reading and history. He "adopted" nearby children to his college residence to help them and their working families. Later upon graduation, Peter returned to live in Connecticut with us. So what did he do in addition to working?

Peter joined Big Brothers and worked with a child whose vision of success was collecting garbage. Peter showed him the opportunities he could create through work and study, thus improving his grades and enjoyment of school. He next took children for their first airplane flight through negotiating free flights for these underprivileged children. The purpose behind this was to provide them with exposure to what the rest of the world does and sees plus to inspire them that they, too, could become pilots or teachers.

While doing this, Peter became the VP of the Greenwich Jaycees. He helped with Habitat for Humanity in refurbishing homes for the needy and elderly. He also became an organizer of breast cancer fund raising and marches in Connecticut and later in Massachusetts.

Later, upon being transferred to the Boston area, he continued working with children to uplift their vision of what they could do and become. He also contributed time to cancer fundraising and breast cancer marches. He became a bone marrow donor and contributed time to a Maine camp for children with cancer.

Peter is now a partner, senior architect for a major software company. He is married to a wonderful and generous wife who is in sales and trains salespeople for her company. Peter has worked for major Fortune 500 companies such as IBM, Putnam and others.

He has been interviewed by newspapers and other media. Articles appeared about his charity work beyond his success in business. What Peter told the interviewers was that he came from an advantaged childhood. He grew up in a beautiful and prosperous community where the high school was more than equal to the finest prep schools. He had the advantages of luxury cars, money, and great care and participation by his parents in all that he and his brothers did. But what he wanted to emphasize was that both of his parents had worked hard to arrive where they were in life and taught him that life is more than taking. It is through the act of giving back of one's talents that one truly is blessed and fortunate in all one does.

To this day, Peter does all in his power for

friends, neighbors, his community and anyone in need while keeping to his strong sense of ethics and personal responsibility. Proudly, I can add that he is one of four fine men who are similar in this regard.

Richard J. Anastasi, New York

My father always told me, "It doesn't cost anything to be friendly." He was always waving and saying hello to people he didn't know. His other expression was "Smile, and the world smiles with you. Cry, and you cry by yourself."

He died on March 15, 1994.

Scott Bloom, New York

We've all heard to be nice, etc. But maybe the best piece of advice was that "the worst thing you can do to another person is to embarrass him." Meaning that other than the obvious, that is, making fun of him, etc., sometimes you must let someone else pay; or too much (or ill timed) flattery can be bad.

Dewey Shay, New York

My father, to me, within days of his death:

Enjoy women—women are wonderful.
Take care of your mother.
You are a good boy.

Howard John Shay died December 26, 1972.

Senshu Ye, China

1) If your coworkers (or boss) tell you that your part of a project is not good enough, try to improve it. If you don't know how to improve, ask your coworkers or your boss. Don't take the complaint personally.

2) If you find a teamwork job has fault, try to find your part first. Make sure that you have done your part perfectly, then talk to other team members.

3) If you don't get along with a person, ask yourself if you have done anything wrong toward him/her. If that person doesn't get along with other people either, it probably is not your fault. If you don't get along with more than one person in one place and they get along with others, it's time for you to adjust. If, from place to place, you don't get along with people, you need to consult your friend(s) who get(s) along with people quite well. Newspapers like the *LA Times* and magazines like *Reader's Digest* may help you understand other people and cultures.

4) If you are hurt by a person, try to calm down and don't jump to conclusions. Be considerate, try to think what you would do/say if the roles of you and the other person were switched. Maybe he/she already regrets what he/she said or did to you but doesn't know how to apologize, or

he/she didn't mean it the way you think. For we ourselves hurt others unintentionally or by mistake from time to time.

In short, handle your job carefully and treat people magnanimously.

Jeff Newman, California

There will always be someone bigger and stronger than you. Sometimes you will be the lion and sometimes you will be the mouse; act like the good lion and you will always have a mouse for a friend. Don't hit anybody smaller than you.

Bill Mirbach, USA

Leon Mirbach to Bill Mirbach:

You know what a bore is? Someone who talks about himself when you want to talk about yourself. You want people to think you're smart, charming, and delightful to be with? Get them started talking about themselves, then keep asking relevant questions that keep them talking on the same subject. They'll end the evening singing your praises to their friends. Extra credit: remember some things they said, and ask about the details next time you see them.

Always wear a shirt to the dinner table. *Jim Stengel, Ohio*

Read Mark Twain, not *Mad* magazine. *Jim Stengel, Ohio*

Studying Latin and playing the trombone is good preparation for life. *Jim Stengel, Ohio*

Think at least two seconds before speaking. *Stuart Pardau, California*

Humility has the unique characteristic of disappearing when displayed. *Neal Greene, California*

Think before you act, not afterwards. *Dhiraj Bhattacharya, India*

I'll always remember my dad telling me that you shine the backs of your shoes as well as the front because you want people to think the same of you when you are coming and when you are going. *Charles Cassidy, Massachusetts*

Be kind to all those people you work with on the way up; you never know when you may need them again. *Grant Mosey, Australia*

You have two ears and one mouth; use them in that proportion. *Grant Mosey, Australia*

Here's my dad's "recording": The most important thing in life is to pick your friends well. *Warwick White, Ireland*

The rewards for trusting people are higher than the penalties for not trusting them. *Chris Jacobi, Germany*

Before starting to argue, consider: he may be right. *Chris Jacobi, Germany*

What you see is what you get. *Chris Browning, Georgia*

After you talk to anyone, the only thing you need is that they feel they have dealt with quality. *Scott Ewart, England*

Ninety-nine percent of your happiness will be dependent on who you marry—choose wisely. *Scott Ewart, England*

You always get more flies with honey. So be nice to others and they may just be nicer to you. *Brooks Bonnot, Georgia*

Treat everyone at work with respect. This includes the janitors, who often know a lot more than you think about what is going on. *Alan Cork, Minnesota*

Don't let your children get too friendly with your parents. They'll develop a common enemy. *Rick Bradt, New York*

"To thine own self be true" is a platitude. *Meyrick Payne, England*

Conscious faith is freedom.
Emotional faith is slavery.
Mechanical faith is foolishness.
Meyrick Payne, England

As for my dad, here's a couple of the things he told me:
"Life's not a race, and there's no finish line. Don't worry about competing with other people, what they do or don't, just do what you think makes sense for you."

"A man does his job. He doesn't talk about doing it." *Manu Rana, India*

Son, you may not inherit my money, but you will my great judgment of people. *Dennis Cott, Florida*

"ALWAYS STAY CLOSE TO YOUR BROTHER COME THICK OR COME THIN"—repeated regularly for forty years at the appropriate intervals. *Bruce Gelb, New York*

You never know them until you marry them. *Dave Jennings, Connecticut*

How are you going to get a job with that earring? *Jim Kreider, California*

Worst advice: "Shave your beard off if you want to get on in business." (I never did and I have.) *John Ceserani, England*

Trade-offs

Sacrifices

Advice received by Peter Bradt from his father
(September 2000, Santa Monica)

Things often come down to understanding what you want and what you are willing to give up to get it.

Figuring out what you want is the easy part. If there weren't any tradeoffs, getting more of what you want would always be a good thing. The hard part comes when you have to figure out what you're prepared to give up.

This year's exams are important. They will be the last major grades universities see and will, therefore, play a significant role in your university applications. All else being equal, you would certainly want the best grades you can have. But, you need to decide what you are willing to give up to get those grades.

This is very different than last year. Last year, the pressure was off. It was a chance to notice and appreciate all the wonderful things Winchester has to offer. The tradeoffs were less substantial.

There is no doubt that you have the capability to do almost anything you want. But you need to make choices. Choose to give up a lot to get awesome grades. Or choose to give up a little less to get slightly less than awesome grades. Either choice is fine, just so long as you're making a conscious choice—and understanding the likely consequences of that choice.

Barry Mitchell, New York

My dad has always led by example, but this is one anecdote I still laugh about. When I was a senior in high school, I announced to my dad that I had saved enough money to buy a used car.

He thought that would be a great idea, because now I would not need to borrow his car. He even agreed to take me to the used car lot in town. As we were en route to my new purchase my father had two questions:

1) What kind of car did I want?

2) Since I had this newfound wealth—after buying the car, did I still have enough money to pay for college?

My response was one of complete surprise— "Pay for college? Who said anything about paying for college?"

Dad's response was, "If you have the money to buy something as frivolous as a car, then you must have the money to pay for college."

I guess you can figure that I never did buy that car.

The take-away: Focus on what is important, ignore the frivolous, and spend money on things that really matter!

Rich Bond, Connecticut

My younger son was a good athlete but a poor student. We were sitting out on the porch one day and he asked if we were going to sell the house when he went to college. "Why do you ask?" I said.

"Well, I'm just wondering where I'll come home to when I come home from college for vacations."

I thought for a while and said, "You know, I was thinking about the same thing. It's a big old house and maybe it's too big for your mother and me to rattle around in by ourselves. But then, I realized that with your grades, you're probably going to the local community college and will need a place to stay."

A couple of hours later he sought me out and asked if I was kidding. "No," I said. "Sending a child to a high-end college is like buying a small BMW and driving it off a cliff—each year. Unless your grades pick up, you'll be at community college."

The good news is that he got the message, reapplied himself to his studies and just finished his first year at a fine high-end college with a 3.5 average.

Peter Davis, England

The best thing my father ever did to me was to bribe me not to smoke.

He had to judge the right point at which to dangle the bait. For me that was about age 14, when I had not started to smoke behind the bicycle shed, but I had learned the value of money. So he promised me £100 (a small fortune in those days to a teenager) if I did not smoke till I was 21. There was an annual personal declaration, when he looked me in the eye and asked me to confirm that I was still in line for the prize.

I won it, and found that £100 was nothing like as much as I had expected seven years before !

So my two boys got the same treatment. Except I had to put up £1000 for each...and they wanted it invested in a savings account for the duration...and they wanted the interest.

And they won the prize too!

Corey McGuire, Texas

Upon my worrying about how I am going to be able to pay my enormous monthly school loan payments, my father, Ernie McGuire, gave me some words of wisdom:

"You know, Corey...sometimes I too wish I would have been born to wealthy parents...instead of such damn good-looking ones."

Michael Copeland, England

The day before I went in the Army, my father, who was a career Army officer, gave me the following advice: The hardest part about being in the service is having to take orders from people who are most likely not as smart as you are. And the trick is to accept that as a part of life.

In retelling the story it doesn't seem like a very profound statement. In fact, it sounds a bit arrogant. But the fact is that this piece of advice has served me throughout my adult life. There's some kind of Zen lesson there about accepting that which you cannot change. Or maybe it just means…if you have a problem with authority, avoid the Army and find a way to become self-employed!

John Planalp, Ohio

Mark Twain once said, "I always tried never to let schooling interfere with my education." I was in a job interview once and was asked what was the best piece of advice my dad had ever given me, and all I could think of was that quote by Mark Twain. So I stole it. I'm sure he would have said that.

Bob Cole, New York

Here's a piece of fatherly advice I was given twenty or so years ago. Some academics might find fault with the counsel, but it proved helpful and accurate.

After teaching a basic PR course as an adjunct professor at several area colleges, I was asked by Pace University if I'd like to teach a Marketing 101 course, too. I accepted the offer, but was somewhat dismayed to subsequently find out that I had to use a 400-page, somewhat dry, marketing book as the course text. I wasn't used to teaching based on what another person wrote (the basic text for my PR course was one that I had written) and wondered if it might be an onerous task.

"It's no big deal," my father told me. "Simply read the chapter or chapters you're going to cover the night before the class and you'll know more than your students, who probably won't look at the text until a week or so before the final exam. Share some of the highlights from the text in 10 or 15 minutes, then cover the subject matter from your perspective as a person who's dealt with it."

It worked. The students were more interested in my real life experiences with the subject matter than what the textbook said, and their assessments of me at the end of each semester placed me in the top five percent of faculty in terms of student evaluations.

So much for the value of artsy fartsy text-books.

Calvin Walters, California

I am 43 and have a twelve-year-old son, and my father was a successful businessman of the 60-90's model. We moved frequently and felt that the only really deep conversations we had was on his deathbed—he died at 56 (I was 31). What I notice most is that I need his advice and wisdom now more than ever.

I have taken it on to write letters from time to time with my son to try to pass on some of the bigger ideas in life. At twelve he does not always get it, but I hang on to them after he reads them. Should I get hit by a beer truck one day, he may value these thoughts in harder times.

My father and I had several good, big times together (hunting, fishing, etc.)—but few small ones. I remember asking once about his stocks (as a kid you don't realize what you're asking) and investments—because I wanted to be closer to him (that was a big part of his world) and because I wanted to learn from him. He really misunderstood the request and the intention. I wanted to know about him and spend time with him. He thought I wanted to know about HIS money. His response set us back a bit.

He was a great people person otherwise, and his biggest fear was having no one show up at his funeral (and this was before he got sick). That was the way he looked at the world.

I think as a father I spend more time trying to get my kids to understand the Whys of life, not just the results. I try to be an active teacher, not just a lecturer. I think our fathers were so results-oriented they forgot we did not have their years of experience. Unless we can connect the dots for our kids, they will have to learn the lessons the hard way.

Finally, I believe faith is a powerful thing that fathers can pass on to their sons and one of the things we think least of or know how to do. It is usually so much more feminine. But our fathers all pass away and we need something bigger than them to survive.

Stephen Young, Pennsylvania

When I joined the workforce after college, my father gave me some advice about drinking during lunch. He told it was never a good idea, but if I *was* going to drink at lunch, to make sure I drank whiskey, not vodka. That way at least they'd smell the whiskey on my breath and know I was drunk, not stupid.

Steve Shanck, Michigan

My father, and his before him, grew up on Long Island sound and were big boaters. As I was growing up (in Michigan at that point) he passed this attraction along to me, and I have ever since been very much involved in on-the-water activities.

Whenever I have talked about buying boats (I have had several) I am always reminded of what my father told me on this topic. This may be something he heard somewhere, but every time I tell the story it always gets a chuckle.

"Son, there is only one thing better than owning your own boat. That is *knowing* someone that owns a boat!"

John-Paul Duffey, California

One thing that I'll never forget from my dad was the time I was giving him a hard time for making a donation to some charity when his eight kids were in need of this or that... his response was very simple. "Son, never hesitate to help others, even when you think you need it just as much as them. Whenever I give, I receive tenfold in return." I can't tell you how often I think of that when having to make the decision to help someone in need.

Eugene Shen, Texas

My father taught through example, not words. He always worked really hard, but still spent a lot of time with us. He'd take us to University of Houston football and basketball games. He'd help us build model rockets.

Partly as a result of this, both my brother and I spend a lot of time with our kids. I always got the feeling that my dad was there for me. He always made time to give me advice.

Carry a big stick. *Jorge Pedraza, New York*

Hard work and long hours never hurt anyone. *Alan Cork's grandfather, Minnesota*

Take care of your gear and your gear will take care of you. (Lots of camping in the old Meugniot family.) *Jason Meugniot, California*

If the mind is weak, the body will suffer. *Mike Cuffe, California*

If you're going to be dumb you better be tuff! *Mike Cuffe, California*

Don't work for money. Get money to work for you. *Grant Mosey, Australia*

You can only sit in one chair at a time. (On material wealth.) *Bob Middlemiss, Virginia*

Who pays? *Meyrick Payne, England*

Real estate is about three things—LOCATION —LOCATION AND FINANCING! If you can get into waterfront property—you'll outperform everything. *Patrick Meyer, Connecticut*

In the long run, financial success/independence is not achieved by merely having a good job; you must buy/own assets or securities that have the potential for dramatic appreciation. *Jack Lowden, New York*

How to make a million dollars? Got to work! *Chuck Lieppe, New Mexico*

You can do anything to which you set your mind. *Matt Bud, Connecticut*

Never take my last beer. *Ed Bancroft, Illinois*

"Son, if you decide to be a drunk, for God's sake, drink whiskey. There's nothing more pathetic than a wino." *Brian Dunn, California*

Go to school. My dad was an eighth grade dropout who worked two to three jobs at a time to pay for my education. *Fran Linnane, Georgia*

Hard work is a prerequisite, rather than a guarantee of success. *Samuel Miller, California*

Keep your knives razor sharp. (He was a chef.) *John Ceserani, England*

Manhood doesn't wash off in dishwater. *Bob Middlemiss, Virginia*

Finish the Job

Journey

Advice received by Peter Bradt from his father
(August 2001, Santa Monica)

> *"We shall not fail or falter; we shall not weaken or
> tire. Neither the sudden shock of battle nor the long-drawn
> trials of vigilance and exertion will wear us down. Give us
> the tools and we will finish the job."*

—Winston Churchill
Radio speech, 1941

This year you are going to have days that are
sheer joy, days when everything is going your way
and when it would be impossible to imagine a
better way to spend your time. You are also going
to have days that feel like part of a "long-drawn
trial" that you cannot wait to get out of. My advice
to you is finish the job.

Just as life is a journey, its various stages are
journeys on their own. And sometimes, like our
drive last week through the Santa Monica Moun-
tains, we take a journey for the sake of the journey
itself. Sometimes, we take a journey to get some-

where, to get through to the next stage. This year and the year after at Winchester are both. You should enjoy the time for the enjoyment of the experience itself. You should also be conscious of the time as something that sets up the next journey.

And you need to finish the job to set up the next journey best. From the heat of the trial it's hard to see what the value of the trial is. Looking back you will be extremely glad you finished—not just for the sense of accomplishment, not just for the credibility it gives you in others' eyes, but also for the tools it will give you to take advantage of future opportunities and finish the next job.

Three people appeared to be doing similar tasks. When asked they said:

I'm setting type.

I'm printing a book.

I'm helping to educate our children.

Finish the job. You're not studying for exams. You're not getting an education. You are preparing yourself for the rest of your life. The better prepared you are, the more you'll get out of it. This stage of the journey has a clearly defined end point. My advice to you is to stay committed to reaching that end point, while milking the experience for all that it is worth.

John J. Colletti, New York

When I was twelve my father owned a grocery store in Brooklyn, where I would work a couple of days a week after school. Twelve was an age of daydreaming. When it wasn't about girls it was about how I could get rich or famous with the smallest amount of effort. When I asked my father, who came to this country from Italy with no money and wound up owning his own business and some property, he said that the answer was simple—"just do that which no one else wants to do—and do it well."

I've thought about his advice over the years and by my own observation confirmed that what he espoused was true. Screen actors are very well paid and yet they will act pretty silly at times, something almost all adults just won't do. Starbucks got started by someone who had the nerve to charge $3.95 for a cup of coffee when it went for less than fifty cents, something most people wouldn't have tried. Politicians get elected by kissing babies and sucking up to contributors without the shame that most of us won't endure.

My father's inventions, new for the 1950s, were to extend credit to the then-declining neighborhood citizenry, sell individual cigarettes for two cents each from the pack, and from those particularly hard-pressed he would take dogs, birds, old pianos and such to clear overdue accounts. The neighbor-hood grew to love and respect my father—words that are not usually associated with business. By taking his own advice he was able to outlast a Bohack's supermarket that had opened up across the street from his small grocery store. The management of Bohack's were amazed that that little Italian grocer across the street prospered while they couldn't make a go of it—but of course, my father was doing something that they just wouldn't do—and still don't!

Richard Gelb, New York

Everything I know about how to sail a boat (and, now that I think about it, Life) I learned from my dad.

1. Navigate point to point even when visibility is good… the fog can roll in unexpectedly.

2. Reef early ahead of bad weather. Practice putting a reef in your mainsail before you need this skill.

3. Do the work… and have fun.

4. Many times what looks like the shortest distance between two points takes longer.

5. Study the current charts often… Sometimes you have to wake up really early if you want to get where you're going.

6. Laugh out loud with family and friends.

7. (When it's really important): Sometimes you have to yell.

8. Go to bed early.

9. Always eat a nutritious breakfast.

10. Be careful when you're doing the heavy lifting—protecting your back is easier than recovering from a back injury.

11. Share your life with someone you love… someone you like being with (and can laugh with) who knows how to cook.

12. Check the anchor right before you sleep (and also if you wake up in the middle of the

night)—sometimes your trusty anchor can drag in the night.

13. It may not always be convenient, but make it a priority to eat a lot of salad, vegetables & fresh fruit.

14. Pump out the bilge often.

15. Do regular maintenance and make all necessary repairs.

16. Stay alert: Check under the sail often—watch for hazards, approaching boats, the unexpected rock, etc.

17. Watch for lobster pots when the engine is on—it's easier to avoid a buoy than to spend an hour trying to disentangle rope from a propeller blade.

18. Enjoy/savor the quiet moments of being together as a family.

19. Get away from phones, TV and newspapers for weeks at a time.

20. Clean up as you go.

21. Don't pollute.

22. Don't eat the last peach (or cookie)—share food with others.

23. Always bring books—after the work is done … read

24. If you're feeling sick…take a nap.

25. Enjoy the journey.

Luis Urrutia, Pennsylvania

I was born in Cuba and came to this country as a refugee in the early '60s. My father left everything behind so he could give his children a real chance in life.

I have always been very driven. In high school, I was involved in just about every extracurricular activity while getting super grades. I was up for an award freshman year but another student got it because of political connections. I was extremely disappointed. My father told me that there would always be circumstances where the deck was going to be stacked against me for some reason or another. And I had a choice to make: either complain and live a bitter life or realize the world was not fair and get on with life. If I chose the second road, I would be much more likely to live happily and reach my potential. I took his advice and went on to experience a very rich and rewarding time in high school….And, I ended up getting that same award, but as a senior, not a freshman, which was the truly coveted recognition. I have come across more experiences in my life than I can count where that advice came in handy.

What makes this remarkable is that it came from a man who, at the age of forty-five, left all his worldly possessions to start anew in a country where he didn't speak the language, couldn't practice the career he loved, and had to start his profession all over again as if he had no experience. And he never missed a day of work, demanded excellence from himself and his children, and always painted a vision of the great and boundless opportunities ahead.

L. Jay Tennenbaum, California

When Harry was in his final days with colon cancer, I tried to pep him up by saying, "Pappy, you can lick this damn thing." He responded by saying, "I'm no fool and know they are going to shovel me soon but I HAVE NO REGRETS. I have had forty great years with your mother, played all the golf I could play and drank all the booze I could hold. If they let me out of this I'd just do the same old thing all over again."

The advice: "Son, someday they are going to shovel you just like they will me, but I have no regrets, so live your life making decisions so that on that day you will look back with NO REGRETS."

So I gave Goldman Sachs notice, as I felt Gretchen and I would be happier with my devoting more time to her. It was a decision based on my dad's advice to have NO REGRETS—and I have none.

Tom Kontos, Indiana

"Work hard for your money so your money can work hard for you." That's one of my favorite one-liners from my dad, Theodoros Kontorousis, now Terry Kontos.

As far as a story goes, my dad's story as a Greek immigrant is the one I recount most often. He was a merchant marine for a Greek shipping company and disembarked in New Orleans for a furlough. In those days, the company allowed its employees to journey in the U.S. to take another of the company's ships for another voyage from any U.S. port of call. He traveled to New Jersey and one of his cousins convinced him to stay in the U.S. He went to work at that cousin's diner in New Jersey. By the time the immigration authorities caught up with him some years later, he had gotten married, started a restaurant business, had a home and a car, and had my sister. If he had been deported I might have been born in Greece!

Instead, the immigration authorities who came to visit him in his restaurant recognized that this was a good tax-providing and employment-providing citizen, and they allowed him to travel to Canada in order to apply for his visa from out of the country (as you're supposed to). He then went through Americanization and became a U.S. citizen.

Mark Gault, England

The vast majority of my father's advice was focused on cricket, which is likely to be of scant interest to most of you.

Otherwise, in keeping with his sporting inclinations, he talked frequently about life as "the greatest game"...where winning is nice, but taking part in the fullest and most involved way is much more important.

(Mark died in 2003 in his mid-forties. He left behind two young children and a lot of people that remember his taking part in life to its fullest all the way.—GBB)

Bob Viney, Connecticut

I asked my dad for advice on where to go to college, and what to select as a major. Of course, I was hung up on the importance of these choices to my future, at the age of seventeen. My dad's advice was, choose to go where you feel there's a great fit, and choose to study any subject about which you are passionate, or at least one in which you find it easy to do well. For you will achieve at the highest levels where you are passionate about the subject, and there you will find it easy to spend the time to do well. And the reward of success is a powerful reinforcement for your efforts.

So I asked him then, what if I choose wrong, and find out later I want to change colleges or majors? His response was that as long as I amassed a record of success and achievement in whatever I did, I would find that I would have all options and choices open to me at any point in the future. In other words, focus on achieving success in whatever I was doing in the present, and the long term would take care of itself.

This advice turned out to be pretty important in my own life. At the time (1966) there was not the expectation that most people would likely change jobs, even careers, multiple times in the course of their lives, but with my dad's advice I didn't worry about making a wrong choice. I had been interested in following my dad into a career as a submarine officer, so I accepted a nomination to the Naval Academy and worked for four years to gain acceptance to the nuclear power submarine program—which required successfully passing a personal interview with Admiral Hymen G. Rickover, the father of the nuclear Navy.

But six years into that career, I determined that the Navy was not the future I wanted any longer. Because of my achievements to that point, however, I successfully passed an interview at P&G for the Brand Management program, and without any background to that point in business, traded in my nuclear power expertise to sell coffee and detergents to America's consumers.

I have since passed the same advice on to my own sons. My eldest chose to attend Penn, where he could play sprint football, a NCAA Division I sport that follows all the rules of traditional football with the exception that players cannot exceed 165 pounds at a weigh-in before each game. He studied political science, because that was his passion at the time. He developed an interest in drama, acting and film production at Penn, and now works as a producer at NFL Films, where he is able to make his living engaged in his two current passions, football and film production.

I hope this advice works as well for my younger son.

Len Ganz, New York

My father always told me that anything in excess was no good. Too much wine. Too much whiskey. Too many women. I, on the other hand, told my sons three things:

1) play the piano
2) dance
3) don't get married until you're 30

Playing the piano would be a constant source of joy.

Learning to dance pleases women. As much as boys don't want to learn to dance—they think it's "faggy"—it makes a big impact on women later in life.

I got married when I was 21—too young. We still didn't know who we were, let alone were we ready to bond with someone else forever. We got divorced.

At this point, my sons have not learned to play the piano, have not learned to dance and are both over 30 and not married. I'm not sure if this is because they're following my third piece of advice or because they've missed out on their perfect mate because of a lack of musical and dancing ability.

Steve Carples, Minnesota

The first thing that came to mind was my father saying: "Never take a job for the money... other than sleeping, the next biggest investment of your time is work. You got to feel good about what you're doing." I've tried to remember this as I have made choices throughout my career.

Peter Wolf, Louisiana

My father was a cotton broker. What he liked to tell me as business advice was "talk, trade and travel." What he meant is, after you have concluded whatever, don't linger.

Mark McDermott, New York

I grew up with four boys. My dad's advice to us included the following:

• Do college in four years—straight or you're paying for it on your own.

• Don't smoke. (He was a chain smoker.)

• Call your mom on Sunday nights because traditionally that has been our family day

• Encourage, no—*make* your kids have a summer job throughout high school so they learn the value of money early on, and so they have their own spending cash.

• Give your kids a modest allowance and make them save it. They can use it to buy something they really want, not just spend it on everyday items.

• Treat everyone with respect, regardless of who they are.

• When somebody tells you that you can't (are not able to) accomplish something, prove to yourself you can—if it is important to you.

• Place your family first, before anyone and anything else.

• Always keep your self-esteem, and take pride in yourself.

• Always remember, all your hard work will soon pay off.

• Make sure you get to know your kids' friends' parents.

• Keep close to your kids so they don't get misguided by others.

Meyrick Payne, England

- Tell your young children what to do.
- Encourage your teenagers to do the right thing.
- Ask the right questions of your adult children.

Sandy Rogers, Missouri

I have had the good fortune of having both a father and a stepfather.

The best advice I've gotten from my father is to watch out for people who are "all necktie and no underwear."

The best advice I've gotten from my stepfather is "no risk it, no biscuit."

Steve Wilde, Connecticut

It was after my sophomore year at a highly competitive college in southern California. My father knew I stressed over tests and papers. Before I left our Connecticut home my dad told me that college just may be the most fun I'd ever have—close friends around, almost always available "to play," living in a very different culture with lots of time to explore and enjoy. And it all ends upon graduation.

Well, from then on I didn't get uptight about the work—I just did it. And I made sure I got around southern California and had fun with friends...with whom I now have to call or e-mail to stay in touch.

Wisdom from Dad added incalculable joy and learning to those final two years.

When cooking, clean as you go along. That way the kitchen is not a wreck when dinner is ready. *Victor Boyce, California*

Best advice I got was on cars 25+ years ago—change the oil regularly and keep tires inflated/in good shape, and the car will last. *Jim McPartland, Connecticut*

Don't be incapable of correction. *Dhiraj Bhattacharya, India*

"Success is the mother of failure." Similar to explanation of the opposite saying; a man can be led to failure if he thinks he has succeeded and needs no more those good characters who brought him to success from failure. Clinton is an example! *Mike Fei, Taiwan*

Best piece of advice I got from my father was to pick something you like doing and do it well...and to do something you enjoy. Otherwise life is too short. *Matt Ariker, Ohio*

If you can't figure out what you want to do in life—figure out jobs you don't want to do. *Patrick Meyer, Connecticut*

Golden Rule: The man with the gold makes the rules. *Sign on the wall behind Harry Kangis' father's desk, Greece*

Allow anyone three chances to let you down. After that they have struck out. *Scott Ewart, England*

Don't be too disappointed when things do not go your way. There is usually a reason for it not happening. It is called fate and you cannot do anything to change it. *Brooks Bonnot, Georgia*

Do not procrastinate. *Brooks Bonnot, Georgia*

Don't throw away the avocado pits...they make good plants...if you like sticks. *Rick Bradt, New York*

"If you can keep your head when all about you are losing theirs" and remember everything else in Rudyard Kipling's famous poem. *Meyrick Payne, England*

Run Through the Tape

Completion

Advice received by Peter Bradt from his father (August 2002, Amagansett)

My high school track coach and friend, Mark Mullen, like every other track coach there ever was and ever will be, demanded that we run through the tape. So many potential winners are passed at the last second as they look around to see how they did, break stride too early, fail to stretch for the finish line or relax in anticipation of finishing. The discipline Coach Mullen taught us was to finish the race five yards beyond the finishing tape. We would literally run through the tape as though it wasn't there.

Running through the tape is about focus, detail, and enthusiasm. As you go through your last year at Winchester, it's important to be mindful that it's not over until it's over. It doesn't end with university applications. It doesn't end with university acceptances. It doesn't end with exams. It ends with the final Domum dinner. It's a wonderful place and a wonderful experience. It's in your best interest to stay focused on the learning and the experience through the entire year.

Completing a task is about completing all its details. I often find myself wanting to leave part of a task until later. But then I stop and say to myself, "Don't be lazy." Whether it's cleaning my flute after using it, putting the cover on my car or spell-checking an important presentation yet one last time, the task isn't complete and I haven't run through the tape until I've handled every detail.

There's a saying that you get out of something what you put into it. It's not good enough to complete a task. If you don't do it with enthusiasm, gusto and energy, you won't do it as well as you could and you won't get out of it all that you could.

So don't get passed at the end of the race. Don't let distraction, lack of attention to detail or apathy keep you from running through the tape and making your time at Winchester everything you hope it can be.

Morris Bradt Jr., Tennessee

When my father was teaching me to shoot a gun, he emphasized that you should never point a gun at something unless you were planning to actually shoot it. He then added, "The same applies to life. Don't start anything unless you plan to finish it."

Kip Knight, California

The best advice my dad gave me was my first year at summer camp. It lasted for two weeks and the parents came to visit you at the end of the first week. It had been a pretty miserable first week, since I was the smallest kid in the camp and the bigger kids were picking on us smaller types. I was ready to get the hell out of there.

But my dad told me that while I was free to go, I might want to stick it out because things just might get better and I'd be sorry if I wasn't here to enjoy it. And so I decided to stick it out. And come to find out, the second week was a lot better than the first. So much so that I went back to the camp for the next three summers and ended up as a counselor.

So... I got a valuable lesson on the persistence that would come in handy later on in life.

Jim Jordan, Connecticut

I was young. I returned from a year in Vietnam and joined my company as a sales representative feeling pretty good about my capabilities and prospects, even though selling was not exactly what my folks had sent me to college to learn. Nonetheless, in my first year selling chemicals, I enjoyed some successes, met some challenges, and built some promising customer relationships. I cherished those relationships because, even as a rookie, I could see clearly that they were likely to be the currency of my business future. It was one of these relationships, or at least the damage done to it, that prompted a very profound conversation with my father.

The toughest goal I set for myself that year was to break an account that had frustrated our company for years. The account history read like a B movie script. Dropped balls, miscommunications, poor trial runs, even a heart attack had contributed to the fifteen-year drama of failure, that is, until I took the case. In one short year, I swept away all the doubt and put us on the path of righteousness....at least that's how I saw it. I had secured a new trial, a new lease on life. My company (and I) was poised for greatness. Naturally, when my customer, my new best friend, called me in, I assumed it was to place the necessary orders and establish the trial details. Graciously, I invited my boss to join me, ostensibly to lend me his experience, but really to watch me shine.

A few days later, waiting confidently in my customer's tastefully furnished, but business appropriate conference room, my boss and I were trading clever observations of what I had done right to get to this place in history, when my customers' technical director walked in with all the relevant decision-makers and one lab technician in tow. It was the technician who captured my immediate attention. He was pushing one of those rolling tables with the samples we had sent our customer for testing neatly arranged on it. That's when I had my first inkling that my boss wouldn't be buying me dinner that night.

You see, we were trying to sell this customer a liquid chemical with an India ink-like consistency and color. What Ron, the tech, was rolling in looked more like a light-colored bodily fluid, and when the technical director deposited it on the cookie sheet he placed in front of us, we learned that it poured like one also. Some cretin at headquarters had shipped the wrong samples! I was humiliated. The only thing that went right that day was when they gave the cookie sheet to someone else to clean.

Happily for the sake of my psyche, shortly thereafter I was able to go home to my family for Thanksgiving and a generous helping of sympathy for my suffering at the hands of those faceless nincompoops back in the lab. At the Thanksgiving dinner table, when my father, who had started his career in chemical sales, asked how the new job was going, I launched into a diatribe about my misfortune and a scathing editorial about the appropriate punishment(s) for those responsible.

Dad listened patiently, as the wine warmed and the turkey cooled, with a deeply troubled look on his face. As the narrative went on, though, I noticed that his face began to lighten, and by the time I finished, he had an irritating, borderline smirk on his face. I paused to ask, "You find this funny?" He went from smirk to full-blown smile and responded, "A little." Measuring my words in order to preserve the dignity of my position as family grace-sayer for the meal, my mouth said, "Why?" while my face said other things.

Dad pondered the question for a minute, then posed quizzically, "Have you ever stopped to ask yourself, if everything went perfectly, who the hell would need you?" To this day, I still have trouble swallowing cold turkey.

Epilogue: Early in the New Year, after hand-carrying new samples and aided by some great people from the home lab, I watched with confidence as the postponed trial came off without a hitch. I bought dinner that night.

Mike Faught, California

One piece of advice I recall my father having given me (and believe me, they were few and far between) was a quote by Ken Dreiden (I think). He left it for me as a note on my mirror after I won a big student/athlete scholarship in high school. It said: "He who is satisfied with what he has done will never become famous for what he will do."

No congratulations, attaboys, or slaps on the back from this guy. You'd have to know him.

David Cunn, Connecticut

My father taught me that I could succeed in anything that I tried no matter how adverse the circumstances. A great example of that comes in the form of yet another fishing story. My dad worked six days a week, so time with him was precious. On my sixth birthday my dad started an annual tradition of going deep sea fishing on a party boat from Sheepshead Bay. Even though I hated fishing, I went because it was a chance to spend time with him.

One trip that still sticks in my mind was around my tenth birthday. We went out on a day when the seas were quite stormy. I was green three minutes after the boat cleared the dock. My father insisted that I stay above decks and fish even though I was sick as a dog. "Be a man," he said.

All of a sudden, the rod bends and the reel starts to spin out. I had caught something! ...At that exact moment my breakfast decided to do a reverse trip. My dad encouraged me to overcome the seas, the seasickness, and the fish. The result of my efforts was a double hooking—a sand shark and a good-sized flounder. The flounder won the pool on the boat and paid for us to go to an expensive seafood dinner that night with the family.

Without dad's encouragement, I would have

given in to the seasickness and never won that pool, something that I still remember fondly. In fact, I probably would never have gone fishing again. I have never forgotten the lesson of that day; I never quit no matter how difficult the situation. Heck, I even still go fishing (from a pier or a lakeside) and don't get seasick (that much).

Son, when you are the first one in the office in the morning and the last one to go home you will not have any surprises. *Tom Wilen, Ireland*

The harder you work, the smarter you get. *Frank Pedraza, Colombia*

Do what you say you are going to do. *Ralph Coolman, California*

Throw the ball higher on your serves. *Parker Robinson, California*

Hang in there. It's too easy to quit. *Jim Kreider, California*

The power of compounding interest. *Jim Kreider, California*

How Stupid Would You Feel?

Mistakes

Advice received by Peter Bradt from his father
(August 2003, Stamford)

A lot of times the consequences of your choices are uncertain. One sophisticated way to evaluate those choices is to look at the expected rewards and risks of the potential outcomes. Another way is to look at the pain associated with the worst possible outcome you can imagine. Then, think about how stupid you would feel if that outcome came to pass.

Suppose, for example, you were trying to choose between two possible routes: route A and route B. Route A had the potential to get you to your destination in 30 minutes or had the potential to get you there in 45 minutes if you hit traffic. Route B might get you there in 20 minutes. But, if there was rain, your car would slip off the hill and tumble down a cliff. So, how stupid would you feel if the trip ended up taking 45 minutes? How stupid would you feel if you wrecked your car?

As you head off on the adventures associated

with your gap year, you're going to make a series of choices: about where to live, how long to stay, who to associate with, how to spend your time, where to travel, etc. Applying the "how stupid would you feel?" test will help you avoid those choices that could have consequences you don't want to have to deal with.

Many of those relate to things that could do you permanent damage. Having too much to drink in a neighborhood pub in London might lead to a headache. Getting caught transporting drugs across national boundaries might lead to an extended prison term. Getting your wallet pick pocketed in a crowded area would be inconvenient. Getting stabbed in a dark, deserted alley is a different situation.

This year is one of those rare chances to relax and enjoy the experience. You don't owe anyone anything and no one will ever check to see how well you did. It's all up to you. Enjoy it. Milk it. And think about avoiding those choices that could make you feel really really stupid.

Greg Galvez, Mexico

My dad is one for giving great and frequent advice (sometimes, when you don't even need it). Seriously though, one of the best pieces of advice that my dad ever gave me was when as an adolescent I kept coming to him with problems that seemed to be huge at the moment. He advised me to take a little time (a few days) to ponder my next step; that often patience and fighting the urge to react immediately to a situation was a big benefit. What's more, if it involves other people, they often can't do the same and they end up acting first, often to their detriment. I have remembered this advice over the years and I've learned to use time as my ally during tough situations.

Norbert Vonnegut, South Carolina

When my dad was growing up, he was one of fifteen people who sat at the dinner table every night. There were nine siblings in his family, four cousins who lived with them because a tragic accident had taken their parents, and then my grandparents, of course. (As an aside, some of the cousins move to Tahiti, where they sold used cars. No sh—. Extended Catholic family…)

My dad was the second youngest and protective of his younger brother, Paul. One day at school, another kid thrashed Paul in a playground fight, so my dad said he would settle the score. He chased the younger kid the next morning before class and didn't catch him. He chased the kid during recess and didn't catch him. He chased the kid after school and caught him. The kid beat the sh— out of my father, and later grew up to win the Golden Gloves championship for the welterweight division in California.

I'm sure that my father's message changed every time he told the story. I think the main headline is "Beware the sure thing."

Abhi Kanitkar, Iran

One item I learned from my father was "While driving, always creep and crawl." While backing up the car, even if you've turned and checked behind you, back out the car at a crawl's pace. It's not a matter of if, but only when, another driver will come tearing around a corner and strike you, or a small child who is below your field of vision or hidden may be in harm's way. Crawling out most often transforms calamity into a near miss—success in this case.

Likewise, when approaching an intersection to make a turn, always creep up to the intersection, pause to check traffic and then turn. Too often, cars that "roll" into the intersection get struck by other drivers who may be tearing around a corner or trying to run a yellow light.

Blair Taylor, California

This first piece of advice did not come from my dad, but from an old Amherst College colleague who was also a former gridiron teammate of mine. Upon hearing the news of the birth of our third child, he quickly remarked to my wife and me: "Taylor, looks like man-to-man coverage won't work anymore. Gotta go with the zone-D." Needless to say, Bridgette and I have perfected the "1-1" zone-defense in our attempt to hold our own ever since.

The second piece that comes to mind actually did come from my dad. It had to do with finances. He said, "Remember, you can never go broke making a profit." It is interesting that perhaps more than anything I learned in business school, that one comment has helped calm my Monday morning quarterbacking on many a real estate or stock transaction (when you make money, but second guess yourself later).

Frank Bacchus, New Jersey

When my son was around seven years old, we got involved in soccer. I would spend a lot of time coaching the team and became the Commissioner of Soccer for Holmdel (recreation). When my son was nine years old, I created a separate soccer club in the township to foster and grow higher levels of talent in the community. This club, dubbed the Stallions, became part of the "travel" community.

At the time, I guess I thought it was a noble thing to do (form the club, etc.), but looking back, as much as I was doing this for all the kids, I was doing this for my son (and my daughter). My life was spent around soccer with the club and with the kids. I always thought that my son was enthusiastic about playing and I would do anything to get him to games, tournaments and other soccer events. I was possessed.

When he was thirteen, we were on vacation in Hawaii and my son announced that he was not going to continue playing. At first I thought he wanted a couple of weeks' break, but he was serious. He just didn't want to play anymore. I couldn't figure it out. I was so upset that I spent about two weeks not speaking with him. After all, I had dedicated all my time and energy while being abused by parents, officials and other coaches. How could he not want to play?

We finally spoke and he held his ground. I asked what he wanted to do instead. He chose playing the guitar. Within three months he had mastered the guitar and within nine months created a local band and cut two CDs. There was a hidden talent which we knew not of. Today, he is 23, just finished college (NYU) and is in the hedge funds business—but still plays the guitar and loves it.

The moral of my story is that as fathers (and parents), we cherish our kids, and we believe that we know what is right for them. But in this case, I was wrong and should have supported his desires from the get go. Sometimes, we need to let go and let them make their own decisions with our support.

Ilan Sobel, Australia

Context: Your son (aged 20+) starts to get serious about his girlfriend.

Father's advice: Make sure you take a real hard look at her mother, because that's what she is going to look like in thirty years...and if you are OK with it then go for it, but at least you know what the worst case looks like.

Harry Blashka, Connecticut

Like most dads, mine, Norman Blashka, was happy to give advice, often ignored, and usually spot on. Having worked as a civil servant his entire career, his views on professional conduct were somewhat different than those usually proffered in the corporate world, but there were times, in retrospect, that a big mouth like me might have been better off if I had followed them.

He would say, "When you get to work, say good morning, keep your mouth shut, do your job, and say good night when you go home." This simple advice, the antithesis of the one about the squeaky wheel, might have prolonged my tenure in a couple of organizations.

Choose your battles wisely! *Craig Reiter, California*

Make sure whatever you do, that you can look yourself in the mirror the next day. *Ross Mohr, California*

Study how it comes apart so you can put it together again. *Ralph Coolman, California*

You can be right, and you can be dead right. *Mike Murray, North Carolina*

Sometimes you can't rub the cat the right way …you have to turn the cat around. *Mike Murray, North Carolina*

Hurry, worry and curry can ruin your health. *Dhiraj Bhattacharya, India*

Never hire a secretary that is better looking than your wife! *Jeff Wahl, Ohio*

Don't ever force anything mechanical. *Dan Kelly's grandfather, August Seher, Georgia*

Never leave anyone you love with a harsh word. You may never get the chance to take it back. *Scott Ewart, England*

When a man loses his temper, he's at the end of

his knowledge. *Bob Middlemiss, Virginia*

You should always have health insurance. *Mike Madden, insurance broker, Massachusetts*

Don't listen to everything your mother says...she makes up a lot of it. *Rick Bradt, New York*

Don't let drunks hold little kids at cocktail parties...they tend to drop them. *Rick Bradt, New York*

You've only got one pair of eyes and feet. Take care of both, and don't spare any expense. *Jim Reichert, New York*

Two can play that game. *Jeff Newman, California*

Cars are the worst investment. They depreciate the minute you drive off the lot. *Alan Cork, Minnesota*

Tools for the Task

Individuals

Advice received by Peter Bradt from his father (August 2004, Amagansett)

As you go off to college for the first time, you're a very different person than you were when you went off to boarding school. And your expectations of what college can do for you should be different than what high school did for you. Just as different tools like hammers and wrenches are appropriate for different tasks, different schools provide different services.

Colet Court and Abberley Hall completed your primary education. Winchester gave you one of the strongest secondary educations in the world. Your base is extremely solid. Penn is about something totally different.

For you, I think Penn is about exploration. There's nothing you need to learn there. There's nothing you have to do. You come in with a wonderful mind and a wonderful set of experiences. I'd urge you to trust your own instincts at this point and focus on the things that feel right. It's a fabulous time of your life. Be choiceful about how you use the time to get the most out of it—however you, and no one else, defines that.

I'm going to give you a copy of Richard Light's book *Making the Most of College*. Key words out of it for me are:

Faculty—Get to know the good ones. You'll learn more from them than from any book.

Students—Get to know a variety of them. You'll learn more from them and the variety of their opinions and perspectives than you will from any class. Study in groups to capture synergies.

Extracurriculars—Engage. Your experience will be richer if you do. Whether it's drama or literary magazines or clubs or sports or…it doesn't matter. Get involved. You'll get back far more than you put in.

Courses—take a variety all along. Don't wait to do the electives.

This is going to be the most fun you've ever had. Enjoy it.

Patrick DeMarco, California

On a funny note first, my dad had a funny but demented saying when I misbehaved. "I brought you into this world and I can take you out of this world." OK. A bit much, but I always got the point.

On a more serious note, I received some excellent advice over the years from my father. Probably the most important thing my father taught me was that FEAR was the major difference why some achieved their dreams and others fell short. He used to joke that fear was the dirtiest four-letter word in the dictionary. To this day I have never really been afraid of failing. It instilled a huge self-confidence that has helped me accomplish a great deal both personally and professionally. Although it may sound rather corny, I truly believe I am "special" and destined for greatness. These feelings of self-esteem and security are rooted from my father and his wisdom.

Sam Perry, California

Just yesterday, a wonderful fellow named Bob Scanlan, who runs a real estate investment company out of Portland, Oregon, told me the following story he'd heard from a good family friend, whose grandfather appeared to be dying in the 1930s. The grandson was about age eight, and his father sent him in to visit with his ailing grandfather in his grandfather's bedroom.

"Granddad, I love you," the son began. "You've lived a long and wonderful life—but if you had anything that you'd have done differently, Granddad, what would that be?"

Granddad thought for a few moments, then looked his eight-year-old grandson in the eye and said: "Grandson, I would have worried a lot less about getting the clap."

My father, who's due to turn ninety on July 9, was always a bit Spartan about advice—but he often carried around in his wallet little nuggets of advice or sayings he'd spotted in a newspaper—some lasted for years.

My favorite, after a poem on the 29-29 Harvard-Yale football tie game he quite liked, was the response of a man who was celebrating his 60th anniversary with his wife to a question as to what he credited their success in staying married for so many years in an era when an increasing proportion of marriages ended in divorce:

"Frequent separations, accompanied by a gradual loss of hearing."

My father was probably not on his 40th anniversary at the time he spotted this, but was nearing retirement and petrified of having to stay at home all those hours with my mother, who had "plans for him," as one might say. They managed to celebrate their 64th anniversary before she passed away last December. I notice that although they rarely separated for more than a few hours in their later years, my father utilized the advice relative to hearing quite effectively! (Especially when instructions were being given to him.)

On the reverse side, my mother and father once asked me in front of guests what I wanted to be when I grew up.

"A man," was my instantaneous and proud reply.

Vera Ho, Hong Kong

NEPALI GOOD LUCK TANTRA TOTEM: INSTRUCTIONS FOR LIFE

1. Eat much brown rice.

2. Give people more than they expect and do it cheerfully.

3. Memorize your favorite poem.

4. Don't believe all you hear, spend all you have, or sleep all you want.

5. When you say, "I love you," mean it.

6. When you say, "I'm sorry," look the person in the eye.

7. Be engaged at least six months before you get married.

8. Believe in love at first sight.

9. Never laugh at anyone's dreams.

10. Love deeply and passionately; you might get hurt but it's the only way to live life completely.

11. In disagreements, fight fairly. No name-calling.

12. Don't judge people by their relatives.

13. Talk slowly but think quickly.

14. When someone asks you a question you don't want to answer, smile and ask, "Why do you want to know?"

15. Remember that great love and great achievements involve great risk.

16. Call your mum.

17. Say "bless you" when you hear someone sneeze.

18. When you lose, don't lose the lesson.

19. Remember the three R's:
  • Respect for self;
  • Respect for others;
  • Responsibility for all your actions.

20. Don't let a little dispute injure a great friendship.

21. When you realize you've made a mistake, take immediate steps to correct it.

22. Smile when picking up the phone. The caller will hear it in your voice.

23. Marry a man/woman you love to talk to. As you get older, their conversational skills will be as important as any other.

24. Spend some time alone.

25. Open your arms to change, but don't let go of your values.

26. Remember that silence is sometimes the best answer.

27. Read more books and watch less TV.

28. Live a good, honorable life. Then when you get older and think back, you'll get to enjoy it a second time.

29. Trust in God, but lock your car.

30. A loving atmosphere in your home is so important. Do all you can to create a tranquil, harmonious home.

31. In disagreements with loved ones, deal with the current situation. Don't bring up the past.

32. Read between the lines.

33. Share your knowledge. It's a way to achieve immortality.

34. Be gentle with the earth.

35. Pray. There's immeasurable power in it.

36. Never interrupt when you are being flattered.

37. Mind your own business.

38. Don't trust a man/woman who doesn't close his/her eyes when you kiss.

39. Once a year, go someplace you've never been before.

40. If you make a lot of money, put it to use helping others while you are living. That is wealth's greatest satisfaction.

41. Remember that not getting what you want is sometimes a stroke of luck.

42. Learn the rules, then break some.

43. Remember that the best relationship is one where your love for each other is greater than your need for each other.

44. Judge your success by what you had to give up in order to get it.

45. Remember that your character is your destiny.

46. Approach love and cooking with reckless abandon.

Ed Tazzia, Michigan

Regarding my father, he was not one for talking a lot. One thing he did show me still works today, especially with groups of kids. If he had a large group that was being unruly, he would say whatever it is he wanted to say and then he'd say, "Really stupid people you have to tell things to three times." By the time he made his statement the second time, the room was generally pretty attentive.

Bruce MacEwen, New York

I'm a child of New York City, and when my parents had driven me to the far yonder of Northfield, Minnesota, to begin my freshman year at Carleton College, as my father was about to get back into the car to leave, his last and parting words were:

"Give 'em hell."

And so I tried.

Jeff Urdang, Connecticut

When I started at KPMG in 1989, my father pulled me aside and, in a very serious tone, said, "If you go out for lunch, don't order the onion soup or a twirly pasta." (The reason, of course, is that neither can be eaten elegantly.)

He also reminded me upon dropping me off at Williams that "As smart as all of these kids are, half are going to graduate in the bottom half of the class."

He also pointed out the absurdity of the Little League exhortation "Throw strikes."

Regarding negotiation: "Don't threaten to walk away from a deal unless you're willing to do it."

Let the other guy waste the gas. *Ralph Coolman, California*

Why worry about something wholesale when you can start worrying retail? *Stuart Pardau, California*

The best advice I received from my father was, "Never judge another person until you walk a mile in their shoes." Somewhat hackneyed, but it's served me well and, in turn, I've been passing the message to my kids. *Bob Johnson, New Jersey*

If you're going into business, make sure you have a monopoly on something that is addicting. *Robin Eichleay, California*

Buy your first house as soon as possible. *Meyrick Payne, England*

Sometimes the Road Isn't Straight

Summing Up

Advice received by Peter Bradt from his father
(August 2005, Amagansett)
(Well, at least partly. This conversation, like the road itself, most definitely did not travel in a straight line.)

Someone once told me that everyone has a plan until they take their first hit. The road isn't straight. You will have to adjust to its turns. It's about mapping out the perfect life and making your life fit that plan. It's about taking the gifts that you're given and making the most of them.

A couple of points to remember:

Conditions, Choices and Consequences —Always remember that I love you no matter what. So far you seem to have made very good choices with the turns in your road. Keep looking down the road to try to understand the consequences of those choices. And, when they go bad, as some will, I'll do my best to help you pick up the pieces.

Notice and Appreciate—In the end, it's not so much about the road you choose, but the people you choose to travel with and how you contribute to their lives and learn from them. Take the time to notice and appreciate them as you do so well.

Trade-offs—You will take hits. You will have to make trade-offs. Learn to live with that and move on.

Finish the Job—It is a journey. And it's a journey with stages. Make sure you're enjoying and getting the most out of each stage or chapter and preparing yourself for the next one.

Run Through the Tape—And make sure you finish each task in its appointed order. You don't want to give up and miss the learning.

How Stupid Would You Feel?—You're going to make mistakes. Sometimes you'll have to choose between two bad choices and often you'll have to choose without perfect knowledge. Make sure you minimize the downside wherever you can and can live with the potential consequences of your choices.

Tools for the Task—In the end, we're all individuals. Be true to yourself and your dreams. There's no one on earth just like you. Treasure the differences and be you.

That's what I know. Have a great year!

Matt Bostwick, Connecticut

The best advice my dad gave to me was how he lived his life and the example he set. Captured in his favorite quote from James Bryant Conant: "Each honest calling, each walk of life, has its own elite, its own aristocracy, based on excellence of performance." He had it framed and gave it to me on the eve of a major heart surgery in 1979. On the back he wrote: "Don't settle for being a prince —Dad 8/9/79." He made it through the surgery and lived fifteen more wonderful years.

I have tried to live my life by that ever since, with uneven success. Whatever the outcome, he did inspire me to never give up and strive to make the most of whatever gifts have been given to me. The picture still hangs in my study. I see it almost every day.

David Raines, Georgia

Well, if advice from Walter Dunn counts, it is among the best I have ever received. When I decided to take the job in Japan, I asked him for advice on how I might be successful there. And he said, very simply, "Be yourself," and it stuck with me the whole time. I followed his advice, and despite the fact that I was a complete failure, I still treasure the advice.

Ray Marschall, Connecticut

My favorite advice from my dad: "You are the captain of your ship. Set a course and adjust later ...don't let someone else take the helm, and don't drift."

Dave McKay, Michigan

My father, George McKay, passed last year, but his wisdom will help guide me throughout my life.

On choosing a career:

"Figure out what you like to do and then learn how to make a little money at it."

On keeping a balanced perspective in business:

"In the past thirty years I've seen business management swing from a focus on the numbers to a focus on people and back. All business is fundamentally about people. If you have the right people in the right places the numbers will come, unless you have too many of the right people; then you have chaos."

"I wish I would have remembered more often that I had a good job to support my family, not the other way around."

"I've worked for visionaries and pragmatists. Visionaries can kill a business before it has the chance to fulfill their vision. Pragmatists can kill a business's future by accepting too many compromises today."

"In most business, success seems to be based on 5% strategy and 95% execution."

Chris Fay, Japan

Most of what I learned from my father was delivered non-verbally. His is the George Bush generation: short on words, long on standards and efforts to meet them. I was the youngest of five children. I cannot recall many instances from my early youth in which my father had information or advice that he wanted to convey only to me. As I grew older, however, and my older siblings left the "nest," my father and I grew very close. Younger children, unlike their older, less fortunate siblings, do not require loads of training. They learn the ropes by watching others (parents and siblings alike) make mistakes. They don't get much tutoring.

Realizing one day that he had never had to teach me much of anything, my father dubbed me "the Oracle," a nickname he made common use of until the day I left for university. Nevertheless, I do recall a few instances in which he said things to me alone and for my benefit. All but the first, third and last are paraphrased.

• "Don't ever, ever in your life, try to understand women." (My dad had just concluded a losing argument with my mom.)

• "Once you start working, you will probably never have an opportunity to stop. Postpone it as long as possible."

- "Always remember, you are a gentleman, and a Fay." (a mantra delivered just before we would go out during high school)
- "Don't worry if you are asked to order the wine for the table. Unless you spend all of your time studying these things, it is unlikely that you will know the vintages on the list. Just know what people are ordering; whittle it down to a few candidates and ask the steward for his final advice. Nobody will care what you order and everybody will be glad that you made the decision—not them."
- "Sport is for exercise and to be with friends. Competition is for bores who get too much of the former and have too few of the latter. Relax and have fun."
- "Try not to say anything about anyone unless you are willing to say it to them face to face."
- "Follow-through on any swing (golf or tennis) is the most important part. Think about this and you will have a much easier time."
- My father makes excellent sandwiches. They are not fancy; not at all. But they taste spectacular. I once asked him to show me how/why this was so: "Both salt and pepper on the mayo and a stacking plan (for lettuce, tomatoes and meat) for the rest. Lightly toasted bread that is fresh."
- "Don't ever do things the way I do." (Basically this is financial advice.)

Ever try? Ever fail? Try again. Fail again. Fail better!
Bob Reilly, California

The older I get, the wiser my father was. *Dennis Cott, Florida*

Postscript

We're all on a journey, a journey filled with choices and consequences, things to notice and appreciate, tradeoffs, tools and advice. I've spent eight years asking people I've met for the best advice they ever got from their fathers. How about you? Got a great story, anecdote, or quip we should know about? Send it to me by e-mail, mail, or carrier pigeon. We'll fit it into a future version of *Back-to-School Chats*.

George Bradt
c/o Durban House Publishing Company
7502 Greeneville Avenue, Suite 500
Dallas, Texas 75231
gbradt@post.harvard.edu

My advice to you:

_____

_____

_____

_____

_____

_____

_____

_____

_____

_____

_____

_____

_____

_____

_____

Contributors

Williams, George, 4
Wolf, Peter, 86
Ye, Senshu, 44
Young, Stephen, 65